PRESIDENTS

JAMES K. POLK

A MyReportLinks.com Book

J B POLK, J. BRA
Bramwell, Neil D. DEC 16 2003
James K. Polk

$19.95

 31994011853766

Neil D. Bramwell

MyReportLinks.com Books
an imprint of
 Enslow Publishers, Inc. E
Box 398, 40 Industrial Road
Berkeley Heights, NJ 07922
USA

MyReportLinks.com Books, an imprint of Enslow Publishers, Inc.

Library of Congress Cataloging-in-Publication Data

Bramwell, Neil D., 1932–
 James K. Polk / Neil D. Bramwell.
 p. cm. — (Presidents)
Includes bibliographical references (p.) and index.
Summary: Traces the life of the eleventh president, who established an
independent Treasury.
 ISBN 0-7660-5052-1
 1. Polk, James K. (James Knox), 1795–1849—Juvenile literature. 2.
Presidents—United States—Biography—Juvenile literature. [1. Polk,
James K. (James Knox), 1795–1849. 2. Presidents.] I. Title. II. Series.

 E417 .B73 2002
 973.6'1'092—dc21

 2001004269
Printed in the United States of America

10 9 8 7 6 5 4 3 2 1

To Our Readers:
Through the purchase of this book, you and your library gain access to the Report Links that specifically back up this book.
The Publisher will provide access to the Report Links that back up this book and will keep these Report Links up to date on **www.myreportlinks.com** for three years from the book's first publication date.
We have done our best to make sure all Internet addresses in this book were active and appropriate when we went to press. However, the author and the Publisher have no control over, and assume no liability for, the material available on those Internet sites or on other Web sites they may link to.
The usage of the MyReportLinks.com Books Web site is subject to the terms and conditions stated on the Usage Policy Statement on **www.myreportlinks.com**.
In the future, a password may be required to access the Report Links that back up this book. The password is found on the bottom of page 4 of this book.
Any comments or suggestions can be sent by e-mail to comments@myreportlinks.com or to the address on the back cover.

Photo Credits: © Corel Corporation, pp. 1 (background), 3; Courtesy of American Memory/Library of Congress, pp. 24, 27, 31; Courtesy of Descendants of Mexican War Veterans, pp. 12, 38; Courtesy of *Harper's Weekly*, p. 33; Courtesy of MyReportLinks.com Books, p. 4; Courtesy of Polk Memorial Association, pp. 19, 20; Courtesy of Town of Pineville, N.N., p. 14; Department of the Interior, p. 29; Enslow Publishers, Inc., p. 35; James K. Polk Memorial Association, Columbia, Tennessee, pp. 1, 17; Library of Congress, pp. 22, 44; National Archives, pp. 37, 40.

Cover Photo: © Corel Corporation (background); James K. Polk Memorial Association, Columbia, Tennessee

Contents

MyReportLinks.com Books
Great Books, Great Links, Great for Research!

MyReportLinks.com Books present the information you need to learn about your report subject. In addition, they show you where to go on the Internet for more information. The pre-evaluated Report Links that back up this book are kept up to date on **www.myreportlinks.com**. With the purchase of a MyReportLinks.com Books title, you and your library gain access to the Report Links that specifically back up that book. The Report Links save hours of research time and link to dozens—even hundreds—of Web sites, source documents, and photos related to your report topic.

Please see "To Our Readers" on the Copyright page for important information about this book, the MyReportLinks.com Books Web site, and the Report Links that back up this book.

Access:

The Publisher will provide access to the Report Links that back up this book and will try to keep these Report Links up to date on our Web site for three years from the book's first publication date. Please enter **PPO1178** if asked for a password.

Report Links

 The Internet sites described below can be accessed at
http://www.myreportlinks.com

*EDITOR'S CHOICE

▶**James K. Polk: His Intentions and Methods**
This Web site provides a unique look at James K. Polk. Here you will
learn about his life and administration through an essay and
conversations with university professors.

Link to this Internet site from http://www.myreportlinks.com

*EDITOR'S CHOICE

▶**The James K. Polk Ancestral Home**
At this site you can explore the home of James K. Polk in Columbia,
Tennessee. You can also read detailed biographies of James and Sarah
Childress Polk, and learn about the key events in his administration.

Link to this Internet site from http://www.myreportlinks.com

*EDITOR'S CHOICE

▶**James Polk: The Manifest Destiny President**
This site provides a comprehensive biography of James K. Polk. Here
you will learn about his life before, during, and after his presidency.
You will also learn about his election, campaign, domestic and foreign
policy, and his legacy.

Link to this Internet site from http://www.myreportlinks.com

*EDITOR'S CHOICE

▶**James Knox Polk, Eleventh President of the
United States**
This site provides facts and figures of James K. Polk. Here you will
find links to Polk's election results, cabinet members, notable events,
historical documents, and other resources.

Link to this Internet site from http://www.myreportlinks.com

*EDITOR'S CHOICE

▶**James K. Polk Is Elected Eleventh President of the
United States November 5, 1844**
This site provides a brief overview of James K. Polk's rise to the
presidency and his commitment to westward expansion.

Link to this Internet site from http://www.myreportlinks.com

*EDITOR'S CHOICE

▶**James Polk**
Here you will find links to James Polk's inaugural address, quick facts
about his life and presidency, and a biography.

Link to this Internet site from http://www.myreportlinks.com

Report Links

 The Internet sites described below can be accessed at
http://www.myreportlinks.com

▶**American Presidents Life Portraits: James K. Polk**
Here you will find "Life Facts" and "Did you know?" trivia about James K. Polk. You will also find a letter written by Polk and links to his birthplace and grave site.

Link to this Internet site from http://www.myreportlinks.com

▶**George M. Dallas**
This site contains a brief biography of George M. Dallas, James K. Polk's vice president.

Link to this Internet site from http://www.myreportlinks.com

▶**"I Do Solemnly Swear..."**
Here you can experience James K. Polk's inauguration by browsing through letters and documents describing the arrangements for Polk's inauguration.

Link to this Internet site from http://www.myreportlinks.com

▶**James K. Polk: Message on War with Mexico, May 11, 1846**
At this site you can read James K. Polk's declaration of war message to Congress.

Link to this Internet site from http://www.myreportlinks.com

▶**James Polk: The Workaholic**
In this brief summary of James K. Polk, author Paul Bacon describes Polk as a workaholic. At this site you will also find an original document and a video clip.

Link to this Internet site from http://www.myreportlinks.com

▶**James Polk's Twenty-five Volume Diary**
At this site you can read pages from James K. Polk's diary.

Link to this Internet site from http://www.myreportlinks.com

Report Links

➤ **The Internet sites described below can be accessed at http://www.myreportlinks.com**

▶**James K. Polk**
This profile of Polk comes from the *North Carolina Encyclopedia,* maintained by the State Library of North Carolina. It traces Polk's rise in politics and discusses his accomplishments as president.

Link to this Internet site from http://www.myreportlinks.com

▶**James K. Polk (1795–1849), Eleventh President (1845–1849)**
The National Portrait Gallery holds the portrait of James K. Polk, painted by Minor K. Kellogg. You will also find a brief description of Polk's presidency.

Link to this Internet site from http://www.myreportlinks.com

▶**James Knox Polk**
Bartleby's vast collection of electronic documents contains James Knox Polk's inaugural address, delivered on March 4, 1845.

Link to this Internet site from http://www.myreportlinks.com

▶**James Knox Polk (1795–1849)**
Here you will learn about Polk's life and his role in gaining territory for the United States.

Link to this Internet site from http://www.myreportlinks.com

▶**John L. O'Sullivan, "The Great Nation of Futurity" (1845)**
The concept of Manifest Destiny was first introduced by journalist John L. O'Sullivan in this editorial published in 1845.

Link to this Internet site from http://www.myreportlinks.com

▶**Manifest Destiny**
This site traces the history of the concept of Manifest Destiny. You will also find an examination of how Polk and others used Manifest Destiny to justify the westward expansion of the United States.

Link to this Internet site from http://www.myreportlinks.com

Report Links

➤ The Internet sites described below can be accessed at
http://www.myreportlinks.com

▶ **The Napolean Stump**
Here you will learn how James K. Polk came to be nominated by the
Democratic Party. You can also read Polk's nomination acceptance letter.

Link to this Internet site from http://www.myreportlinks.com

▶ **Objects of the Presidency**
By navigating through this site you will find objects related to all of the
United States presidents, including James K. Polk. You will also find a
brief description of Polk and the era he lived in and learn about the office
of the presidency.

Link to this Internet site from http://www.myreportlinks.com

▶ **Polk, James K.**
At the Encyclopedia.com Web site you will find a brief overview of James K.
Polk's early career and presidency.

Link to this Internet site from http://www.myreportlinks.com

▶ **Polk, James K(nox)**
At this Web site you will find biographical information about James K.
Polk and other United States Presidents. You will also find links to
important documents.

Link to this Internet site from http://www.myreportlinks.com

▶ **President James Knox Polk**
Here you will find a profile of James Knox Polk, along with an interesting
fact, a quote, events in his administration, and his inaugural address.

Link to this Internet site from http://www.myreportlinks.com

▶ **Treaty with Great Britain, In Regards to Limits Westward of
the Rocky Mountains**
Here you will find the text of the Oregon Treaty. This treaty resolved the
Oregon Territory dispute between Great Britain and the United States.

Link to this Internet site from http://www.myreportlinks.com

Report Links

▼ The Internet sites described below can be accessed at
http://www.myreportlinks.com

▶ **The U.S.-Mexican War**
This site brings the Mexican War to life. Here you will find images,
maps, documents, and historical information about the war.

Link to this Internet site from http://www.myreportlinks.com

▶ **Welcome to Pineville North Carolina**
This site provides a biography from James Knox Polk's birthplace,
Mecklenburg County, North Carolina. Also included are quick facts
and trivia about Polk.

Link to this Internet site from http://www.myreportlinks.com

▶ **The White House Historical Association**
At the White House Historical Association you can explore the rich
history of the White House and the presidents of the United States.
You can also take a virtual tour of the White House, visit the
president's park, and experience past presidential inaugurations.

Link to this Internet site from http://www.myreportlinks.com

▶ **The White House: James K. Polk**
The official White House Web site holds the biography James K. Polk.
Here you will learn about Polk's accomplishments as president.

Link to this Internet site from http://www.myreportlinks.com

▶ **The White House: Sarah Childress Polk**
The official White House Web site holds the biography of
Sarah Childress Polk. She played an active role in her husband's
political career.

Link to this Internet site from http://www.myreportlinks.com

▶ **Who is James K. Polk? The Enigma of Our
Eleventh President**
Here you will find a speech titled, "Who Is James K. Polk? The Enigma
Of Our Eleventh President," given by Robert W. Johannsen at the
Tenth Hayes Lecture on the Presidency.

Link to this Internet site from http://www.myreportlinks.com

Any comments? Contact us: **comments@myreportlinks.com** 9

Highlights

1795—*Nov. 2:* James K. Polk is born in a log house in Mecklenburg County, North Carolina.

1806—The Polk family moves to Tennessee.

1813—Enrolls in school for the first time at age eighteen.

1816—Admitted as sophomore to University of North Carolina at Chapel Hill.

1818—Graduates from University of North Carolina; moves to Nashville, Tennessee, to work for Felix Grundy, a prominent lawyer and political figure.

1819—Chosen clerk of the Tennessee state senate.

1820—Passes the bar exam and begins practicing as an attorney in Tennessee.

1823–1825—Serves as a member of Tennessee House of Representatives.

1824—*Jan. 1:* Marries Sarah Childress.

1825–1839—Serves as congressman in the U.S. House of Representatives.

1835–1839—Chosen as speaker of the House of Representatives.

1839–1841—Serves as governor of Tennessee.

1844—Elected eleventh president of the United States. He does not seek a second term.

1846—Agrees to Oregon Treaty, giving the United States what would later become the states of Washington and Oregon.

April: Polk asks Congress for a declaration of war against Mexico.

1848—Treaty of Guadalupe Hidalgo fixes the Rio Grande as the border between the United States and Mexico. The United States receives land that becomes all or part of the present-day states of California, Nevada, Utah, Wyoming, Colorado, Texas, New Mexico, and Arizona in exchange for roughly $18 million.

1849—*June 15:* Dies in Nashville, Tennessee.

Chapter 1 ▶

Texas and the United States, 1845–1846

James K. Polk was sworn in as the eleventh president of the United States on March 4, 1845. Just a few days before his inauguration, Congress had passed a resolution to admit Texas as the next state in the Union. President Polk was not at all surprised that Congress had approved the annexation of Texas. Shortly after he was elected, Polk had authorized his Washington representatives to let it be known that he wanted Texas annexed before his inauguration.[1] He strongly believed that all of the western territory that separated the United States from the Pacific Ocean—from the border with what would become Canada in the north to Mexico's Rio Grande in the south—must become part of the United States. This belief in the right to American expansion from ocean to ocean was known as *manifest destiny.*

Texas formed the largest part of the territory that lay to the west of the United States. The territory of the Republic of Texas was enormous. It included parts of what later became six states: Texas, Wyoming, Colorado, Kansas, Oklahoma, and New Mexico. By 1845, Texas had been an independent republic for almost ten years, having declared its independence from Mexico on December 20, 1835. Mexico never recognized Texas' independence, however, and still claimed it as a province of Mexico. Mexico threatened war if the United States annexed Texas. President Polk disregarded Mexico's threats. Even in his inaugural address, Polk indicated that he would ignore the threats of other nations and go forward with the annexation

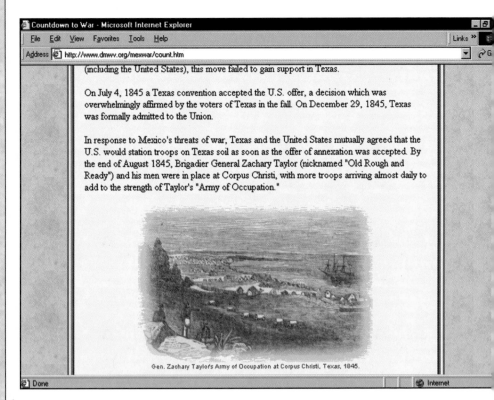

Countdown to War - Microsoft Internet Explorer

File Edit View Favorites Tools Help Links »

Address ❄ http://www.dmwv.org/mexwar/count.htm

(including the United States), this move failed to gain support in Texas.

On July 4, 1845 a Texas convention accepted the U.S. offer, a decision which was overwhelmingly affirmed by the voters of Texas in the fall. On December 29, 1845, Texas was formally admitted to the Union.

In response to Mexico's threats of war, Texas and the United States mutually agreed that the U.S. would station troops on Texas soil as soon as the offer of annexation was accepted. By the end of August 1845, Brigadier General Zachary Taylor (nicknamed "Old Rough and Ready") and his men were in place at Corpus Christi, with more troops arriving almost daily to add to the strength of Taylor's "Army of Occupation."

Gen. Zachary Taylor's Army of Occupation at Corpus Christi, Texas, 1845.

Done Internet

▲ *President Polk sent General Zachary Taylor's army of occupation to the Rio Grande to enforce what he felt was the border between Texas and Mexico.*

of Texas. He declared, "I regard the question of annexation as belonging exclusively to the United States and Texas." He warned, "Foreign nations have no right to interfere with them, or to take exceptions to their reunion."[2]

During the next eight months, the annexation issue was debated in Washington, D.C., Texas, and in Mexico. Polk was determined to annex Texas. Mexico continued to threaten war. Adding to the tension was the issue of the Texas border. Texas claimed the Rio Grande as its southern border, while Mexico claimed the border was much farther north, at the Nueces River. The president backed Texas' claim.

The question of admission of Texas to the Union was debated in a convention held in Texas in July 1845. Mexico offered to recognize Texas' independence if Texas agreed not to allow itself to be annexed by the United States. In October 1845, Texas voted to accept Congress' offer of statehood. On December 29, 1845, President Polk signed the final document admitting Texas to the United States as the twenty-eighth state.

War with Mexico broke out when Mexican troops attacked American soldiers on what Polk believed to be United States soil on the north side of the Rio Grande on April 24, 1846. The soldiers had been sent by President Polk to occupy the land north of the Rio Grande to strengthen the United States' claims that this river formed the border between Mexico and the United States. When Congress received news of the attack, it immediately passed a war resolution and President Polk signed a declaration of war with Mexico on May 13, 1846.

Frontier Boyhood, 1795–1818

James Knox Polk was born on November 2, 1795, near Charlotte, North Carolina. Originally the Polk family was from Scotland. They had also settled for a time in Ireland. James's grandfather and his family had moved to North Carolina from Pennsylvania around 1740, when it was still mostly wild, unsettled country. The Polks were all farmers.

James K Polk History - Microsoft Internet Explorer

File Edit View Favorites Tools Help

Address 🔲 http://www.pinevillenc.net/polk.html ⟳ Go Links

Home

Click on the welcome text above to return to the home page. Click on the town seal to learn more about our history.

JAMES KNOX POLK

(1795 - 1849)

Eleventh President of the United States, 1845 - 1849

James K. Polk was born in Mecklenburg County, North Carolina on November 2, 1795. The Polk family (the original family name was Pollock) came to Maryland in 1680 and gradually moved southward to North Carolina. In 1806, when James was eleven years old, the Polk family moved to Tennessee where James' father was a farmer and surveyor. Young James attended nearby academics and in 1815 entered the sophomore class at the University of North Carolina at Chapel Hill. He graduated in 1818 with high honors.

Polk returned to Tennessee and practiced law until his election as president. His success as a lawyer brought him into politics and his speeches won him the

🔲 🌐 Internet

▲ This is a photograph of the log house where James K. Polk and his nine siblings were born.

The Polk men fought in the Revolutionary War but returned to their farms as soon as the fighting was over.

▶ Patriots

The Polks were strong supporters of American independence. In 1775, James's grandfather, Robert, stood on the steps of a local courthouse and read aloud the Mecklenburg Declaration.[1] It was the first written call for the colonies' independence from Great Britain, and it was issued a year before the Declaration of Independence.

James, called "Jim" for short, was the eldest child of Samuel Polk and Jane Knox Polk. Jim had four sisters and five brothers. His mother was a religious woman. She was from the same family as John Knox, a famous preacher and leader in Scotland in the 1500s. Jim was given his middle name, Knox, in honor of this famous ancestor. All the Polk children were born in a log house built by their father. It was more like two houses with one roof and a hall down the middle that connected them. Big fireplaces at each end of the house supplied heat, light, and fires for cooking. Jim's father was a prosperous farmer who grew wheat, corn, and hemp with the help of his sons and several African-American slaves. Jim, though, was a sickly child, so he did not do much farm work.

Jim and his brothers learned to hunt, ride, and shoot. There was no school, but the children were taught to read and write by their parents. Samuel Polk was often away from home surveying (making maps of) the unsettled frontier country to the west. Jim went with his father on many surveying trips. They traveled through dense forests. Mapping the territory could take weeks. Jim's job was to care for the horses and help cook meals for the surveyors. He also studied the mathematics his father used in surveying.[2]

In 1806, the Polk family moved to Maury County, Tennessee. It was a five-hundred-mile trip west across the Blue Ridge Mountains and the Cumberland Plateau through wild, uninhabited country. The trip took six weeks by horse and wagon. When they got settled in Tennessee, the Polks continued farming. Samuel decided to plant cotton, corn, and tobacco. The family prospered.

▶ A Sickly Child

Throughout Jim's childhood and early adolescence, he suffered from attacks of severe stomach pain. Finally, when he was fifteen, Jim became very sick. His parents decided to send him to see a famous surgeon. The surgeon, Dr. Physick, was in Philadelphia, Pennsylvania, eight hundred miles away. Jim's condition was so serious, that he had to make the trip on a bed set up in a wagon. His parents could not leave the other children and the farm, so Jim went on the journey with his uncle.

On the way, though, he had such a severe attack that he could not go on. Fortunately there was a surgeon nearby, in Danville, Kentucky, who had trained at a very good medical college in Scotland. He specialized in stomach problems. The doctor discovered that Jim had stones in his bladder. He needed an operation immediately. There was no choice. There was no anesthesia either. The only thing the doctor could offer to dull the pain was whiskey. Jim was strapped tight to a flat wooden board so he would not move during the operation. Amazingly, the operation was a success and Jim made a very swift recovery. He and his uncle were able to return home in a few weeks.

▶ Off to School

Back home, Jim's father decided his son was too frail for farming. Instead, Jim was sent to learn shop keeping with a

merchant. Jim hated the work and wanted desperately to go to school.[3] After a few weeks, his father realized he had made a mistake. At the age of eighteen, Jim was enrolled in school for the first time, at the Presbyterian Academy.

After one year, Jim transferred to a bigger school, Bradley Academy. He studied astronomy, mathematics, philosophy, Greek, and Latin. Although Jim studied hard, he also made many friends and still had time for fun. Jim did so well at Bradley that in only two years he was admitted to the University of North Carolina at Chapel Hill as a sophomore.

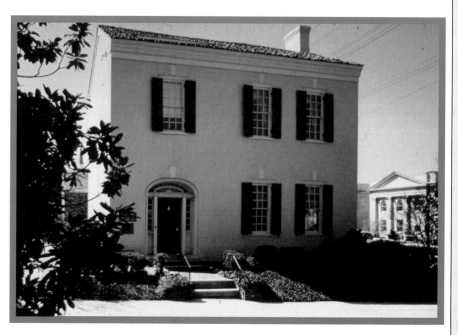

▲ *The Polk Ancestral Home was built by Samuel Polk in 1816. James K. Polk lived here from 1818 to1824.*

Chapter 3 ▶

Pupil to President, 1818–1844

At college, Polk was active on campus and made good friends. He was a serious debater and was elected president of the debate club three times. His college friends included: William D. Mosely, who later became the first governor of Florida; Will Haywood, a U.S. Senator when Polk was president; and John Mason, who would become a member of Polk's cabinet.[1] At his graduation ceremony in 1818, Polk was chosen to give the welcoming address in Latin.

▶ Starting a Law Career

After graduation, Polk returned to Columbia, Tennessee, to visit his family. He had decided to study law and went to work for a man named Felix Grundy in Nashville, Tennessee. Grundy was very influential in Tennessee. He was a criminal lawyer who had never lost a case and was head of the Tennessee Bar, the state's association of lawyers. Grundy was a very good friend of Andrew Jackson, the seventh president of the United States. Jackson was a leading figure in Tennessee politics.

Polk prepared for his legal career the way most lawyers did back then, by doing routine work in Grundy's office. He copied legal papers for Grundy's cases and studied the law books in Grundy's law library. In 1819, Grundy was elected to the state legislature and Polk was chosen as clerk of the state senate. Since the legislature only met for about a month, Polk had plenty of time to study for the bar examination. In 1820, he took the test and passed. Now he

was allowed to practice law in Tennessee. During his time with Grundy, he also got to know the important politicians in Tennessee, including Andrew Jackson.

After passing the bar exam, Polk returned to his family's hometown of Columbia, Tennessee. He told his family that now he would rather be referred to as "James" rather than "Jim" as he began his legal practice. Polk's first case was to defend his father.

Polk's father had lost his temper and punched a man in the nose. Polk lost the case. His father had to pay one dollar plus costs. James handled many cases like this as well as

http://www.jameskpolk.com/bio.html - Microsoft Internet Explorer

File Edit View Favorites Tools Help

Address http://www.jameskpolk.com/bio.html Go Links

Part I

1795-1844

The career of the eleventh U.S. President reflected and fulfilled the young nation's commitment to westward expansion. The son of a North Carolina farmer and surveyor, James Knox Polk was ten years old when his family moved across the Appalachian Mountains. Growing up on the Tennessee frontier, he inherited his neighbors' work ethic, resourcefulness, and democratic ideals.

Done Internet

▲ Polk was a promising young man, who graduated with top honors in mathematics and the classics from the University of North Carolina. Shortly after graduation, he passed the bar exam and served as a clerk in the Tennessee Senate.

small collection jobs. His practice grew and soon he was handling more important land cases. Polk might have continued on this way, slowly increasing his practice. But, one day in Nashville, he ran into Sarah Childress. They had first met at Bradley Academy when Polk was nineteen and Sarah was eleven.

▶ Sarah Childress

Sarah's father was a rich merchant who had sent Sarah to the best schools for a good education. Sarah traveled on horseback two hundred miles away from home across the

Sarah Polk biography - Microsoft Internet Explorer

File Edit View Favorites Tools Help

Address 🔲 http://www.jameskpolk.com/scpbio.htm 🔗 Go Links

Sarah Childress Polk, 1803-1891

Sarah Childress Polk was born in Rutherford County, Tennessee, the third of six children. Although raised in the rugged Western Frontier, Sarah grew up amidst wealth and refinement. Her father, Joel Childress, was a successful businessman and planter.

Although an education was scarce for frontier girls, Sarah attended a local school and was even tutored by area boys' school teachers after class hours. In 1817, both Sarah and her sister Susan were sent to Salem Academy in North Carolina. This school was considered one of the best in the South. The unusually strong curriculum included English grammar,

🔲 Done 💮 Internet

▲ *Sarah Childress was considered a very desirable woman in middle Tennessee because of her ladylike demeanor and excellent education. She was very active in social and political circles, and even assisted her husband in many of his affairs.*

Great Smoky Mountains, accompanied by her father, sister, and a male slave, to the Moravian Female Academy at Salem, North Carolina.[2] Sarah learned the usual skills considered necessary in 1817 for a cultivated lady: fancy needlework, drawing, and piano. However, she also studied arithmetic, grammar, history, and geography. Sarah's family members were close friends of Andrew Jackson. Sarah even called the ex-president "Uncle Andrew." He nicknamed her "Sally." It was Andrew Jackson who advised Polk to get married and backed Polk's choice of Sarah.[3] She promised to marry Polk when he could support her.

James Polk immediately decided to run for the Tennessee House of Representatives. Campaigning was tough: It meant riding across the entire county on horseback, through areas without roads or inns, but the entire area had to be covered in order to reach the most isolated individuals. All of Polk's hard campaigning paid off. He was elected to his seat in the state legislature. He and Sarah were married on January 1, 1924, at his family's home.

▶ Congressman Polk

Serving only one term, Polk did not remain long in the state legislature. Among the people he served with were Davy Crockett and Felix Grundy. In 1825, Polk won a seat in the U.S. House of Representatives. Polk and the rest of the Tennessee delegation traveled to Washington on horseback over the mountains until they reached Baltimore, Maryland. The horses were left in Baltimore until they were needed for the return trip to Tennessee. The journey to Washington was completed by stagecoach.

Polk began his term as congressman during President John Quincy Adams's administration. In the 1824 presidential election, neither Adams nor Andrew Jackson

received a majority of the vote. Therefore, the House of Representatives had to decide the winner. The deciding vote for Adams was cast when Henry Clay, Speaker of the House, asked his supporters to back Adams. On becoming president, Adams appointed Clay secretary of state. Jackson's supporters, Polk included, claimed Clay and Adams had made a dirty deal for Clay's support for Adams. The result was loud and bitter political feelings for the rest of Adams's term.[4] Polk's first congressional speech in 1826 reflected the anger over Clay's vote. Polk proposed an amendment to the Constitution whereby future presidents would be elected by direct vote so that the House of Representatives would never again decide a presidential election. The amendment did not pass. Still, Polk became famous throughout the country as a result of his speech.

Until 1826, Sarah had remained in their two-room log house in Columbia, Tennessee, looking after her husband's affairs. Late in 1826, Sarah joined Polk in Washington where they settled in a boardinghouse for the time Congress was in session. Most members of Congress lived in board- inghouses. Being a congressman was a second job for most members of Congress, because it did not pay very much. Most members returned home as soon as they could to their main jobs or businesses. The Polks lived in boardinghouses most of the fourteen years Polk was a congressman.

Sarah Polk was very active in the social and political

John Quincy Adams.

Tools Search Notes Discuss Go!

circles of Washington. She attended sessions in the House of Representatives almost daily. Sarah's behavior did not always meet the approval of Washington society. Instead of joining the other ladies in the parlor after dinner, she would stay with the men and discuss politics. Accompanying her husband to his office, Sarah acted as Polk's private secretary and political advisor. When Polk was away in Tennessee, Sarah reviewed articles and newspapers and wrote letters keeping Polk informed of events in Washington.[5] She knew, and was liked, by many of the leading political figures of the time.

Jacksonian Democrats

Polk's position in Washington was helped by the election of Andrew Jackson as president in 1828. During the presidential race, Polk campaigned on horseback throughout Tennessee for Jackson. As a congressman, Polk fought for the principles of the party he belonged to, the Democratic Party. Jackson was also a Democrat. The Democrats believed in strong rights and powers for the states and a limited a central federal government. They wanted a federal government that never interfered in anything the states could do for themselves—such as building roads. As far as the Democrats were concerned, the less the federal government had control over citizens' lives, the better. They believed the federal government should only have enough power to defend the country from foreigners. The Democratic Party feared that a strong federal government would concentrate too much power in Washington. A strong federal government, Polk and Jackson believed, might lead to tyranny.

The other national political party was the Whigs. The Whigs believed in a strong federal government. They

feared a weak central government might mean the end of the Union. Later both parties split over the slavery issue. Many of the Whigs living in the North joined northern Democrats to form the antislavery Republican Party. The Democratic Party became mostly limited to the proslavery South. Of course many members of both parties switched parties depending on their beliefs. Tennessee was a border state between the North and the South and therefore was in the middle on the issue of slavery.

▶ The Issue of Slavery

Polk was a slave owner and does not appear to have questioned whether it was right or wrong to own slaves,

Polk was called the "Napoleon of the Stump" by his peers because of his ability to persuade an audience.

although he once referred to the institution of slavery as "mistaken philanthropy."[6] However, Polk had two runaway slaves whipped when they were recaptured and returned to him. Polk feared that the growing abolitionist movement in the North would threaten the compromise on slavery the Founding Fathers had worked out in order to form the Union. He believed that the people living in each state or territory should decide the slave issue for themselves.[7] This belief was known as popular sovereignty.

Polk had seen how the issue of slavery divided the Northern and Southern states. The debate had prevented Jackson from admitting Texas to the Union when it first became independent in 1836. The Northern politicians, led by the Whigs, strongly opposed the admission of Texas. If admitted to the Union, Texas could be carved into five states. The North feared that the five states would all favor the expansion of slavery into their areas. Jackson, afraid of a split between the North and South, refused annexation.[8] There were various compromises that permitted the annexation of the new territories without settling the slavery issue. The slavery issue would not get resolved until the end of the Civil War, over fifteen years after Polk left office.

By 1839, Polk decided to leave Congress, even though he had enjoyed increased power since 1835 when he was elected Speaker of the House. In 1839, the country was in the midst of a severe depression resulting from the Panic of 1837. Many blamed Jackson and the Democrats for the depression because Jackson did not renew the charter of the Bank of the United States and withdrew all the federal funds from the bank. Polk and most of the rest of the Democrats supported Jackson. Polk thought the Bank was unconstitutional and favored big business. Working-class people and farmers—particularly Southerners—thought

the Bank caused high prices for manufactured goods and low prices for farm goods.

Polk was convinced that because of the depression he would not be re-elected Speaker of the House. Moreover, family matters had been especially difficult for Polk. In 1838, his youngest brother, Sam, died from tuberculosis. Another brother was sent to prison for six months. The brother, whose new bride was allowed to join him in prison, was jailed for killing a man in a duel. Finally, Polk was convinced that he stood a good chance of being elected governor of Tennessee. On August 30, 1838, Polk announced that he was leaving Washington to run for governor.

Governor

Polk's campaign for governor was vigorous. He covered over thirteen hundred miles on horseback. Many, if not most, of the roads were muddy tracks across fields and forests, through miles of unsettled land. Polk visited miles of backcountry populated here and there by small farms. Again Polk spoke for the Jeffersonian ideal, favoring small farmers and workers. He favored a lowered tariff for cheap goods and a statewide public school system. Polk emphasized Tennessee's rights as a state and the limits of the federal government. Sarah worked hard for Polk's election, handling Polk's correspondence, arranging his speaking schedule, and doing the political mailings. Polk won, by only twenty-five hundred votes.

As governor of Tennessee, Polk faced hard times financially. The governor was paid little, just two thousand dollars a year. Out of that amount Polk had to pay five hundred dollars per year in rent for the governor's house and all the expenses of the governor's office. The governor received no expense account, and all expenses came out of

Polk's pocket. Polk was forced to borrow money several times to cover the expenses.

In 1840, President Martin Van Buren, a Democrat who had succeeded Jackson as president, was defeated by the Whig candidate, William Henry Harrison. The Democrats were still being blamed for the depression. In 1841, Polk ran for re-election. The voters were angry at Polk for supporting Van Buren. They turned against him and elected James C. Jones governor. In 1843, Polk ran against Jones for governor again, and Jones defeated Polk

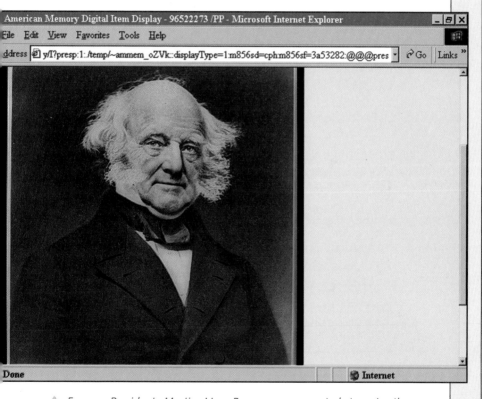

Former President Martin Van Buren was expected to win the nomination for president until a fight developed at the 1844 Democratic Convention between those who supported and those who opposed the annexation of Texas. Polk was not involved in this argument and he won the nomination.

once more. Not only was Polk badly defeated, his Democratic colleagues deserted him completely. During the month following Polk's defeat, he received not even one letter of support from his political colleagues. For the first time in his political life, Polk was silent.[9] James and Sarah returned to Columbia, Tennessee, where Polk returned to his law practice. It seemed as though his political career was finished.

▶ Dark Horse Candidate

On May 27, 1844, the Democratic Convention to nominate the presidential and vice presidential candidates opened in Baltimore, Maryland. Everyone expected former President Martin Van Buren to be nominated as the presidential candidate on the first ballot. However, a fight developed that changed everything. On April 12, 1844, President Tyler announced that he had signed a treaty with Texas to admit Texas to the Union. Again, the issue of slavery split the North and South. The South favored annexation, but the North still feared more slave states would be carved out of Texas. Van Buren tried to delay the issue. He wrote to a leading newspaper that he favored annexation but not until Mexico agreed to it.[10]

As a result, the Convention was split between those for annexation of Texas and those against it. Senator Lewis Cass of Michigan supported annexation. Cass's group at the Convention had been fighting Van Buren for the presidential nomination. The Texas question gave Cass a real chance to gain support. Van Buren could not achieve the two thirds of the vote to win the nomination. After the first ballot, Van Buren continuously lost votes. By the seventh ballot, Cass was the front-runner when the delegates

adjourned for the night. That night the party leaders met. They realized they needed a compromise candidate.

George Bancroft, leader of the Massachusetts delegation, suggested Polk as the compromise candidate. Polk had not been on the first seven ballots and was not involved in the Van Buren–Cass fight. Polk favored annexation and was a close friend of Andrew Jackson, who still had a great deal of influence with the voters. That night, delegates of New Hampshire, Massachusetts, Alabama, and Mississippi all decided to go for Polk.[11] The next day on the ninth ballot, delegates from state after state went for Polk, and he became the candidate. Polk became known as the first "dark horse" presidential candidate—an almost unknown candidate who had come from nowhere to win the nomination. Of course,

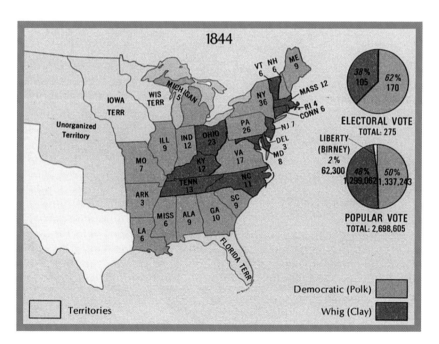

▲ This map shows the results of the presidential election of 1844.

this was not entirely true. Polk had always maintained his political contacts and worked hard to win the nomination.[12]

The great issues of the election of 1844 were the expansion of the United States, tariffs, and an independent treasury. The South favored the admission of Texas, which was opposed by the North. However, both the Northern and Western regions of the country strongly supported taking all of the Oregon Territory.

Polk's campaign linked the admission of Texas with the taking by the United States of all the Oregon Territory, thus gaining the support of all regions of the country. In the North and West, the campaign slogan was "Fifty-four, Forty or Fight."[13] North of the 40th parallel was the Russian territory of Alaska. Great Britain and the United States then shared the Oregon Territory. Great Britain claimed the United States border with Oregon should be fixed at the 42nd parallel. The expansionists wanted all of Oregon at the 40th parallel.

Henry Clay, Polk's opponent for the presidency, at first tried to omit any mention of Texas or Oregon. The North favored high tariffs. A tariff was a tax on imports of manufactured goods that protected the new industries of the North. The South opposed high tariffs since they made the imported manufactured goods on which the South depended much more expensive. Polk campaigned for reduction of tariffs. He also campaigned for an independent treasury that would not be subject to political pressure. The election was close. Polk won a narrow victory of 38,000 votes in the popular vote but had a large margin of victory in the electoral college of 170 votes to Henry Clay's 105 votes. Polk's platform of expansion to Oregon and Texas paid off. George Mifflin Dallas was elected vice president.

The Presidency, 1845–1849

Polk knew exactly what he wanted to accomplish as president. A month after the inauguration, Polk described his aims as president to his secretary of the Navy, George Bancroft.[1] Polk intended the United States to annex Texas, to acquire California and Oregon, to lower the tariff, and to establish an independent federal treasury. All these matters had been fiercely debated during the presidential campaign, particularly the annexation of Texas.

▲ This is a sketch of Polk's inauguration on March 4, 1845, taken from the April 19 issue of the Illustrated London News.

▶ Westward Expansion

The Texas issue came to a resolution when President Tyler submitted a treaty to the Senate that provided for the admission of Texas to the Union. Senate approval required a two-thirds vote of all the senators. The treaty could not get the two-thirds vote. Instead, Congress initiated a joint resolution inviting Texas to join the Union. The congressional resolution needed only a simple majority. The resolution passed both houses of Congress and was signed by President Tyler on March 1, 1845, just in time for Polk's inauguration on March 4, 1845.

Mexico had never recognized the independence of Texas and protested the resolution, breaking off diplomatic relations with Washington. At the same time, the issues of California and Oregon needed attention. Americans had begun settling in both areas. Three presidents—Jackson, Van Buren, and Tyler—all showed their interest in the west coast. San Francisco Bay was considered one of the finest harbors in the world and would be important for trade with Asia. Back in 1835, President Jackson had tried to purchase San Francisco Bay and northern California from Mexico. Mexico refused to sell. President Van Buren had sent a naval lieutenant to visit San Francisco and the surrounding country. The lieutenant was regarded by Californians as a spy for American annexation.[2] Efforts by the United States to purchase California continued until the Mexican War.[3]

▶ Oregon Treaty

The Oregon Territory stretched north from California, all the way to Alaska. At the time, Alaska was owned by Russia. As the result of a treaty signed in 1827, both countries—Great

ULTIMATUM ON THE OREGON QUESTION.

▲ This caricature illustrates the Oregon Question, one of the first major issues of expansion that Polk had to face as president.

Britain and the United States—governed the territory. However the treaty provided that on one year's notice, either side could end the joint occupancy. On February 10, 1846, the United States gave Britain that notice. From that date on, Great Britain and the United States engaged in heavy negotiation over the Oregon Territory. In the presidential campaign, Polk strongly supported the United States' claim to all of the Oregon Territory. Great Britain conceded that part of the territory belonged to the United States but claimed large parts for Britain. To compromise, Britain offered the United States half the area. The United States refused.

Finally, the issue between the United States and Great Britain came down to the northern border of Oregon. The British at first wanted to keep the Oregon border at the latitude of 42 degrees North. This would have given Canada almost all of Oregon, including the Columbia River. The

river was an important outlet to the Pacific. The American expansionists wanted to fight for the northern border at latitude 54°40′ N. This would have sliced off most of the west coast of Canada, leaving it without a harbor and most of British Columbia. Polk, in a great bluff with the British, pretended to support the expansionists.[4] Polk withdrew his offer to the British to settle for the 49th parallel and again demanded all of Oregon as the expansionists wanted. Secretly, Polk had Secretary of State Buchanan assure the British that a compromise offer along with the 49th parallel would be submitted to the Senate for its approval.

In both Great Britain and the United States, there were large numbers of people who opposed any compromise on the Oregon question. There were, however, good reasons to compromise. Many lawmakers had all along seen the latitude 49 degrees North as a realistic border. The 49th parallel, as it is known, gave Britain its western coast on the Pacific Ocean. Still, the United States kept half the Oregon Territory, as well as the all-important Columbia River that ran to the Pacific.

War With Mexico

Almost as important in the compromise was the outbreak of the Mexican War on May 13, 1846. Polk and others were certain that if the United States did not compromise with Great Britain over Oregon, Britain would go to war with the United States.[5] Fighting Mexico and Great Britain at once would have been difficult. Great Britain was then the greatest military power in the world. In the summer and fall of 1845, American officials had delivered to Polk reports of British and French interest in California.[6] In October, Polk received news that Great Britain was pressing the Mexican government to send an

army to California to prevent American settlers there from starting a revolution. There was always the possibility Great Britain would see an opportunity in the Mexican War to take parts of California as well as settle the Oregon question in Britain's favor.[7]

The federal government felt that California was more important to the United States than the northern part of Oregon. Thus, at the time of the Oregon negotiations, there was pressure to compromise before Great Britain used the Mexican War to Britain's advantage. On June 10, 1846, the Senate advised Polk to accept the compromise. On June 18, 1846, Polk's Oregon Treaty with Great Britain was approved by the Senate. The treaty compromised the issues of the Oregon Territory, particularly fixing the

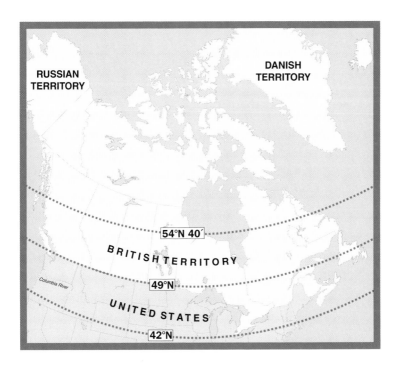

▲ The Oregon Treaty of 1846 set the western border between the United States and Canada at the 49th parallel, or 49°N.

northern border at latitude 49 degrees North. Now Polk could give his full attention to the war with Mexico.

American support for the war with Mexico was mixed. Enthusiasm for the war was high in the Southern and Western parts of the United States. Lawmakers from New England and the North strongly opposed the war. Polk's opponents accused him of starting the war.[8] He answered that Mexico had "shed American blood upon American soil."[9] Behind Polk's words were his intentions to settle the issues of Texas, California, and the $3 million in American claims Mexico refused to pay.

Mexico's anger had been growing ever since the United States invited Texas to join the Union. Two days after Texas became the twenty-eighth state, General Parades of Mexico ordered American Ambassador John Slidell to leave Mexico. Slidell had gone to Mexico to negotiate the Mexico–Texas border. The Neuces River had been Texas' border while Texas still belonged to Mexico. When Texas declared independence, it claimed the Rio Grande, two hundred miles farther west and south, as the border. When Texas joined the Union, the United States repeated Texas' claim for the Rio Grande border. In addition to negotiations over Texas, Slidell was authorized to negotiate the purchase of California and parts of New Mexico. The Mexican government was particularly insulted by the offer to purchase California and New Mexico and refused to see Slidell.

Since the summer of 1845, four thousand American troops under General Zachary Taylor had been stationed along the Nueces River. When he heard that Mexico had ordered Slidell to leave Mexico, Polk decided to apply pressure to Mexico. Polk ordered the troops moved to the Rio Grande. Mexico demanded the removal of those

troops. The United States refused, and Taylor set up a blockade of Mexico. Mexican troops crossed the Rio Grande on April 25 and ambushed an American unit leaving sixteen wounded or killed. Polk signed the declaration of war with Mexico on May 13, 1846.

Polk was an active commander throughout the war, appointing generals and setting strategy. The strategy was not only the annexation of Texas. On May 30, within weeks of the beginning of the war, Polk told his Cabinet the United States should acquire California, New Mexico, and perhaps some other portions of the northern provinces of Mexico when peace was made.[10] New Mexico was annexed with scarcely a shot being fired. The United States Army of the West under Brigadier General Stephen W. Kearny marched all the way to Santa Fe without meeting any real resistance. On August 22, 1846, Kearny, in a proclamation, freed all New Mexicans from their allegiance to Mexico and announced the annexation of New Mexico to the United States.[11]

▲ This image shows the storming of Independence Hill at the Battle of Monterey, one of most severe battles of the Mexican War.

▶ The Fighting Intensifies

California was a different situation. There was severe fighting there. The United States Navy was deeply involved in the war. Monterey, San Francisco, San Diego, and Los Angeles were among the chief coastal towns and cities taken by the Navy in July 1846. While the naval battles were going on, Kearny, led by the famous scout Kit Carson, marched from New Mexico to California. On January 13, Mexico surrendered California and signed the Treaty of Cahuenga.

The surrender of California and New Mexico did not end the war. An invasion of Mexico was necessary. The

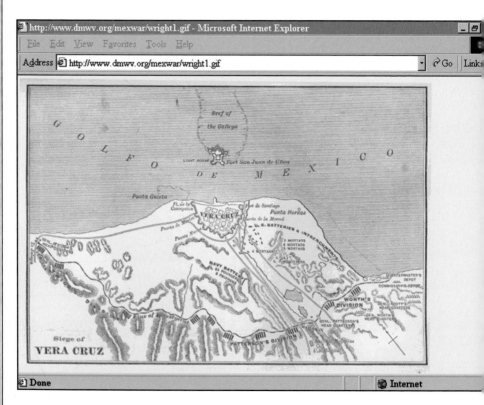

This is a map detailing where American troops invaded and bombarded Mexico's town of Veracruz.

Mexicans fought a long and hard war, continually fighting the better armed and financed invading Americans. For the first time in the nation's history, United States troops invaded by sea from the Navy's ships. The American ships bombed the shore at Mexico's Veracruz, while American troops landed on the beach. American troops, including lieutenants Robert E. Lee, George B. McClellan, and P. G. T. Beauregard, fought their way to Mexico City. It was the first time in history American troops conquered and occupied an enemy capital. The war ended with a battle at Mexico's military academy. Its defenders were young untrained cadets. The battle was over before noon.

Negotiations for peace took weeks. Finally the Treaty of Guadalupe Hidalgo was signed by the Mexican and American governments. Polk achieved all his aims. The Rio Grande became the permanent boundary between Mexico and Texas. Mexico accepted the United States annexation of Texas, California, and New Mexico. The United States had gained more than a million square miles of land. The United States paid Mexico $15 million for its Californian provinces and agreed to assume all American claims against Mexico up to $4.25 million. Fifty thousand Mexican soldiers and thirteen thousand Americans died in the war.[12]

Polk's Other Goals

There remained for Polk only two other major aims of his presidency. He was determined to establish an independent federal treasury and to lower the tariff. The tariff was a charge imposed on certain imported goods by the federal government. The tariff was imposed to make money for the government and to protect American manufacturers from cheaper imported goods. The North, with a lot of

▲ The Americans won the Battle of Molino del Rey on September 8, 1847. They captured the hilltop fortress of Chapultepec. The war ended soon after.

manufacturing, wanted high tariffs to protect its growing industry. The South was mostly agricultural and had almost no manufacturers. The South had to buy most of its manufactured goods from the North or from overseas. The tariff increased the amount the South had to pay for these goods. The South believed tariffs were a burden it suffered for the sake of northern manufacturers. By the Walker Tariff Act of 1846, Polk was able to get the tariffs reduced and applied in such a way that the South no longer felt it was a victim of the Northern manufacturers.

In the same year, 1846, Polk established the Independent Treasury System. Unlike the earlier Bank of the United States, the Treasury was totally independent from all private businesses and state banks. Only the Treasury could handle federal funds and could issue money. All debts to the United States government had to be paid in gold or silver coins or in federal treasury notes.

The Polk administration had other achievements. Polk's signing of the Smithsonian Act of Organization established the Smithsonian Institution. It was built from funds left to the United States by James Smithson, an English scientist who had never been to the United States. When he died in 1829, Smithson willed five hundred thousand dollars in gold to the United States to create an institution for "the increase and diffusion of knowledge among men." Polk attended the ceremony at which the cornerstone was laid for the Smithsonian's first building. Among the last major events of Polk's administration was the establishment of the Naval School in Annapolis, Maryland, on August 15, 1845. Five years later, it was renamed the United States Naval Academy, later to be known simply as Annapolis.

Life as President and First Lady

The president and his wife did not have any children, which allowed them to pour all their energies into the president's office. Mrs. Polk was thoroughly involved with Polk's presidency, as she did not care much for housekeeping. During the presidential campaign, Sarah Polk had been criticized for lack of skills as a housewife. Her answer was, "If I get to the White House, I expect to live on $25,000 a year and I will neither keep house nor make butter."[13] The $25,000 the president was paid did not go very far. Among other expenses, the president had to pay for his office staff, including his private secretary and Sarah's social secretary. Polk's nephew, James Walker, worked as Polk's private secretary. Walker's wife was Sarah's social secretary. All expenses for entertainment came out of Polk's pocket. It was an enormous expense. Entertainment of foreign

diplomats, congressmen, and important people visiting Washington was considered part of the president's duty.

Public receptions were held in the White House on Tuesday and Friday evenings. Each week, elegant dinner parties were given. Music was provided on these occasions, but no dancing or card playing. Mrs. Polk believed they violated her religious beliefs and the dignity of the White House. Mrs. Polk refused to go to the theater or to horse races and did not permit music on Sundays. Sarah Polk was the organizer of all the dinner parties, open houses, and festivities at the White House. She made sure that the events went well—planning all the decorations, choosing the menus and fine wines, and excluding hard liquor. The guest list included the president's political opponents as well as his supporters. Prominent among the guests, and almost always included, was Dolly Madison. Dolly, President Madison's widow, was famous for rescuing Washington's portrait from the White House as the British burned Washington during the War of 1812. Sarah, herself, was well liked in Washington but did not escape criticism for being too controlling and too involved in the presidency.[14] She was sometimes called "Mrs. President."

On his last day as president, Polk worked all day, signing numerous documents. Among them was the document creating the Department of the Interior, which combined many government offices including the Office of Indian Affairs and the Patent Office. That same day, March 4, 1849, the Polks left the White House and moved to the Williard Hotel. The next day, March 5, 1849, Polk rode with Zachary Taylor—hero of the Mexican War—to the Capitol where Taylor was sworn in as the twelfth president of the United States.

The Trip Home, 1849

The Polks began their trip home to Nashville, Tennessee, where they had bought a home for their retirement. The entire tour took a month. The trip began by train to New Orleans and continued by steamboats up the Mississippi and Ohio rivers to Nashville. All along the way, the couple stopped in various cities where they were treated to great parades, dinners, and celebrations. It was an ordeal that wore Polk out. As early as July, Polk had admitted his tiredness and need for a change.[1] By the time he reached Baton Rouge, Louisiana, Polk was too sick to attend the public reception. At Natchez, Mississippi, he suffered from stomach pains, an echo of his boyhood illness. After a short visit to his mother in Columbia, Tennessee, his old hometown, James and Sarah Polk moved into their new home in Nashville.

On June 3, 1849, Sarah was on her way to church when she found Polk lying on the parlor sofa, too sick to attend the service. Doctors came and went, but none could do anything. On June 15, 1849, barely three months after leaving the White House, Polk died. He was buried in the municipal cemetery of Nashville and later his body was moved to the grounds of the Tennessee State Capitol. Sarah Polk lived on, guarding the memory of the president. She lived through the Civil War, losing the family plantation in Mississippi, and in 1882, Congress finally awarded her a pension of five thousand dollars a year. She died in 1891, at the age of eighty-seven.

James K. Polk, as the eleventh president of the United States, added almost a million square miles of territory to the United States. By the additions of Texas, California, and Oregon, the United States became a continental power whose borders stretched from the Atlantic to the Pacific oceans. By reducing the tariffs, Polk helped open the markets to importation of cheap goods from overseas and exportation of American crops and goods to foreign markets. By establishing an independent Treasury, Polk made sure government money was not used for the interests of the private banks and business groups. In its November 16, 2000, edition, the *Wall Street Journal* published the results of its polling of 132 prominent professors of history, law, and political science on the ranking of their presidents from George Washington to Bill Clinton. Seventy-eight of those polled responded. They concluded that President Polk ranked tenth and is included in the "Near Great" of the American presidents.

As president, Polk expanded the territory of the United States and opened the nation to foreign markets.

Chapter Notes

Chapter 1. Texas and the United States

1. Charles Sellers, *James K. Polk: Continentalist, 1843–1846* (Princeton, N.J.: Princeton University Press, 1966), p. 172.

2. John S. Jenkins, *The Life of James Knox Polk* (New York: James M. Alden Publishers, 1850), p. 156.

Chapter 2. Frontier Boyhood, 1795–1818

1. John S. Jenkins, *The Life of James Knox Polk* (New York: John M. Alden Publishers, 1850), p. 25.

2. Ibid., p. 38.

3. Ibid., p. 41.

Chapter 3. Pupil to President, 1818–1844

1. William A. DeGregorio, *The Complete Book of U.S. Presidents: From George Washington to Bill Clinton* (New York: Wings Books, 1997), p. 165.

2. Susan Sinnott, *Sarah Childress Polk* (New York: Grolier Publishing, 1998), p. 21.

3. Ibid., p. 28.

4. Margaret Truman, *First Ladies* (New York: Random House, 1995), p. 95.

5. Sinnott, pp. 44–45.

6. Edwin P. Hoyt, *James Knox Polk* (Chicago, Illinois: Reilly & Lee Co., 1965), p. 79.

7. Miriam Greenblatt, *James K. Polk* (Ada, Okla.: Garrett Educational Corporation, 1998), p. 59.

8. George Brown Tindall and David E. Shi, *America: A Narrative History* (New York: Norton & Company, 1996), p. 581.

9. Charles Sellers, James K. Polk: *Continentalist, 1843–1846* (Princeton, N.J.: Princeton University Press, 1966), p. 6.

10. Ibid., p. 61.

11. Sam W. Haynes, *James K. Polk and the Expansionist Impulse* (New York: Longman, 1997), p. 54.

12. Sellers, pp. 69–70.

13. Ibid., p. 120.

Chapter 4. The Presidency, 1845–1849

1. Charles Sellers, *James K. Polk: Continentalist, 1843–1846* (Princeton, N.J.: Princeton University Press, 1966), p. 213..

2. Alexander De Conde, *A History of American Foreign Policy* (New York: Scribner's Sons, 1963), p. 193.

3. Ibid., pp. 192–194.

4. Sellers, pp. 413–414.

5. DeConde, p. 173.

6. Ibid., p. 197.

7. Sellers, pp. 409–411.

8. George Brown Tindall and David E. Shi, *America: A Narrative History* (New York: Norton & Company, 1996), p. 588.

9. Ibid., p. 587.

10. Sellers, p. 423.

11. K. Jack Bauer, *The Mexican War: 1846–1848* (Lincoln: University of Nebraska Press, 1992), p. 134.

12. Susan Sinnott, *Sarah Childress Polk* (New York: Grolier Publishing, 1998), p. 65.

13. Ibid., p. 53.

14. Ibid., p. 70.

Chapter 5. The Trip Home, 1849

1. Charles Sellers, *James K. Polk: Continentalist, 1843–1846* (Princeton, N.J.: Princeton University Press, 1966), p. 484.

DeGregorio, William A. *The Complete Book of U.S. Presidents: From George Washington to Bill Clinton.* New York: Wings Books, 1997.

Jacobs, William J. *War with Mexico.* Brookfield, Conn.: Millbrook Press, Inc. 1993.

Lawson, Don. *The United States in the Mexican War.* New York: HarperCollins Children's Book Group, Division of HarperCollins Publishers, 1998.

Lillegard, Dee. *James K. Polk.* Danbury, Conn.: Children's Press, 1988.

Lindop, Edmund. *James K. Polk, Abraham Lincoln, Theodore Roosevelt.* Brookfield, Conn.: Twenty-First Century Books, 1995.

Mills, Bronwyn. *The Mexican War.* New York: Facts on File, 1992.

Nardo, Don. *The Mexican-American War.* San Diego, Calif.: Lucent Books, 1999.

Nelson, Anna K. *Secret Agents: President Polk & the Search for Peace with Mexico.* New York: Garland Publishing, Member of Taylor & Francis, Inc., 1988.

Nelson, Anson, Fanny Nelson, and Katherine Speirs., ed. *Sarah Childress Polk: Wife of the 11th President of the United States.* Newtown, Conn.: American Political Biography, 1994.

Polk, James K. *Polk: The Diary of a Presidency, 1845–1849, Covering the Mexican War, the Acquisition of Oregon, & the Conquest of California and the Southwest.* Temecula, Calif.: Reprint Services Corporation, 1991.

Tibbets, Alison Davis. *James K. Polk.* Springfield, N.J.: Enslow Publishers, Inc., 1999.

Welsbacher, Anne. *James K. Polk.* Minneapolis, Minn.: ABDO Publishing Company, 2001.